Asshole

FLOWER SWEAR

Wondrous Swear Word To Color

For Stress Releasing

Charity Borsberry

Happy Coloring!

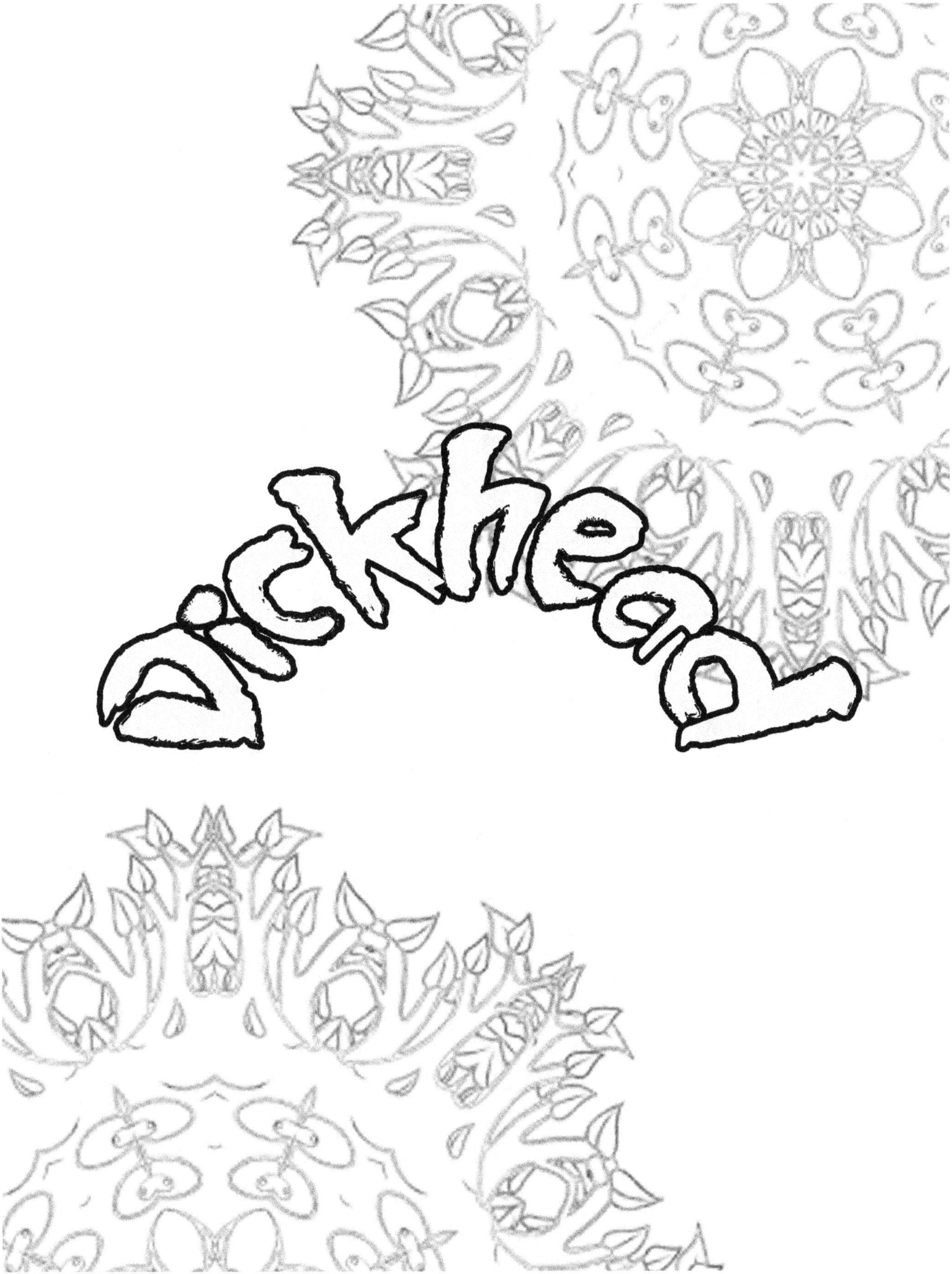
Dickhead

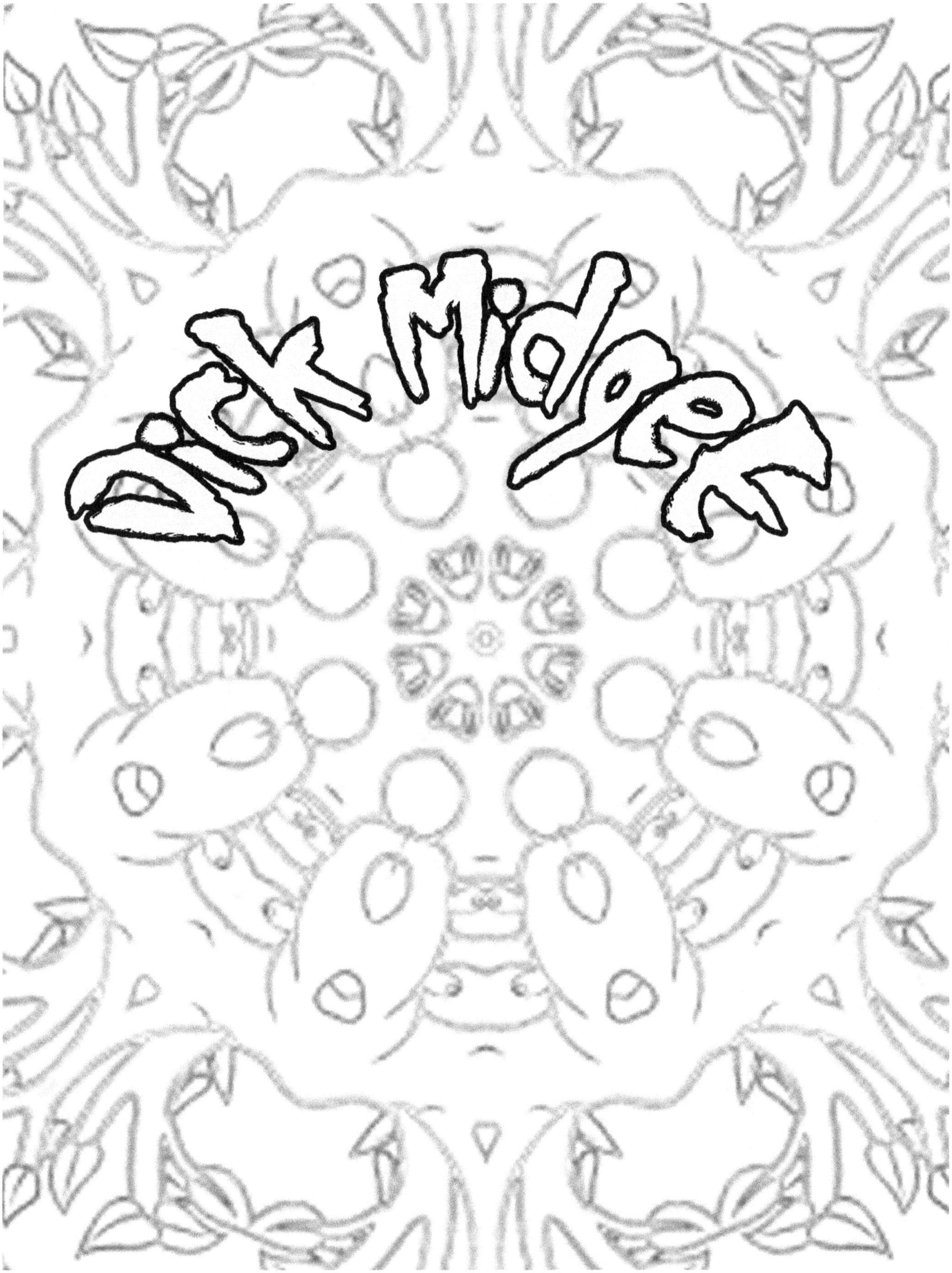
Dick Midget

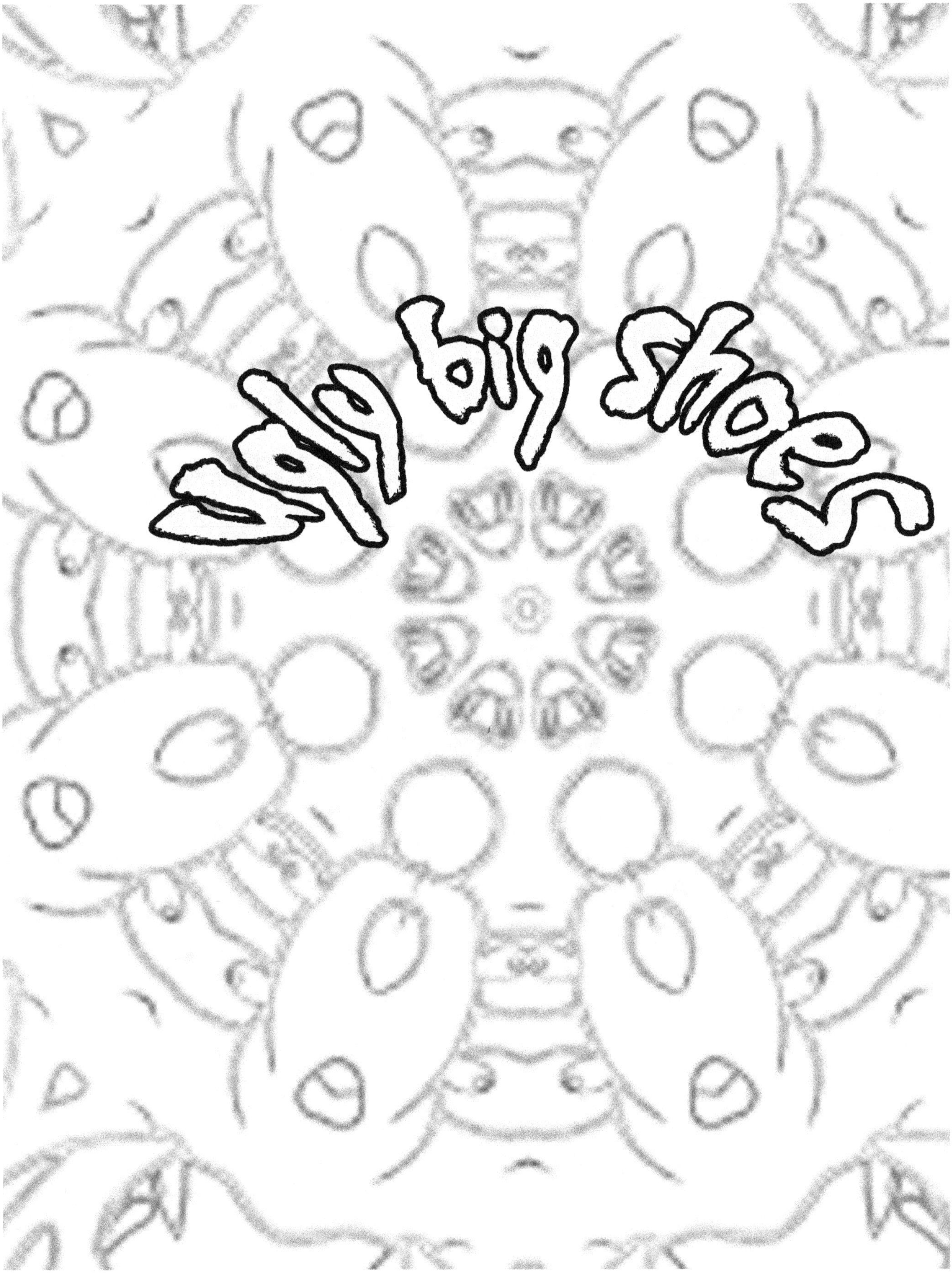
ugly big shoes

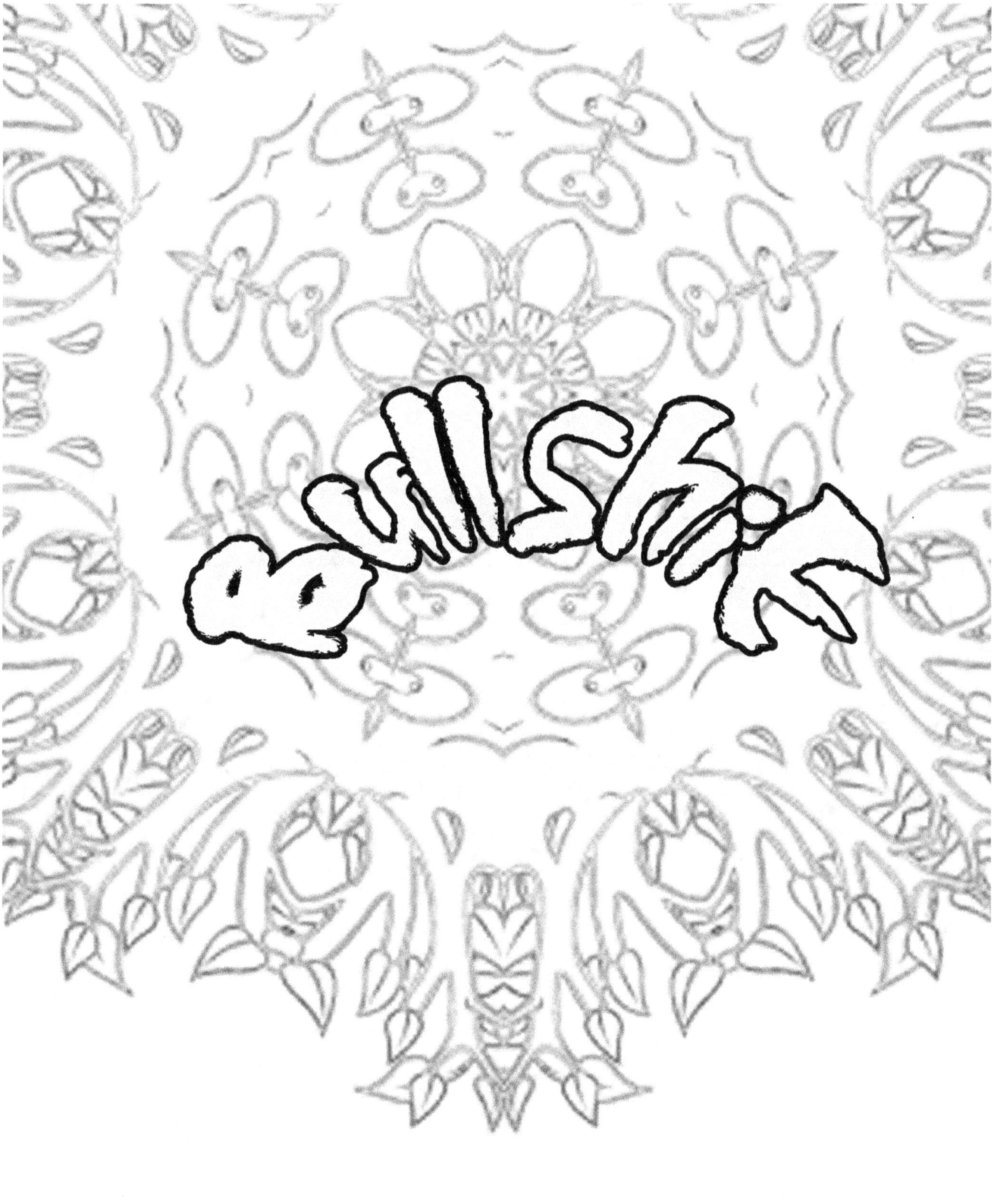
Bullshit

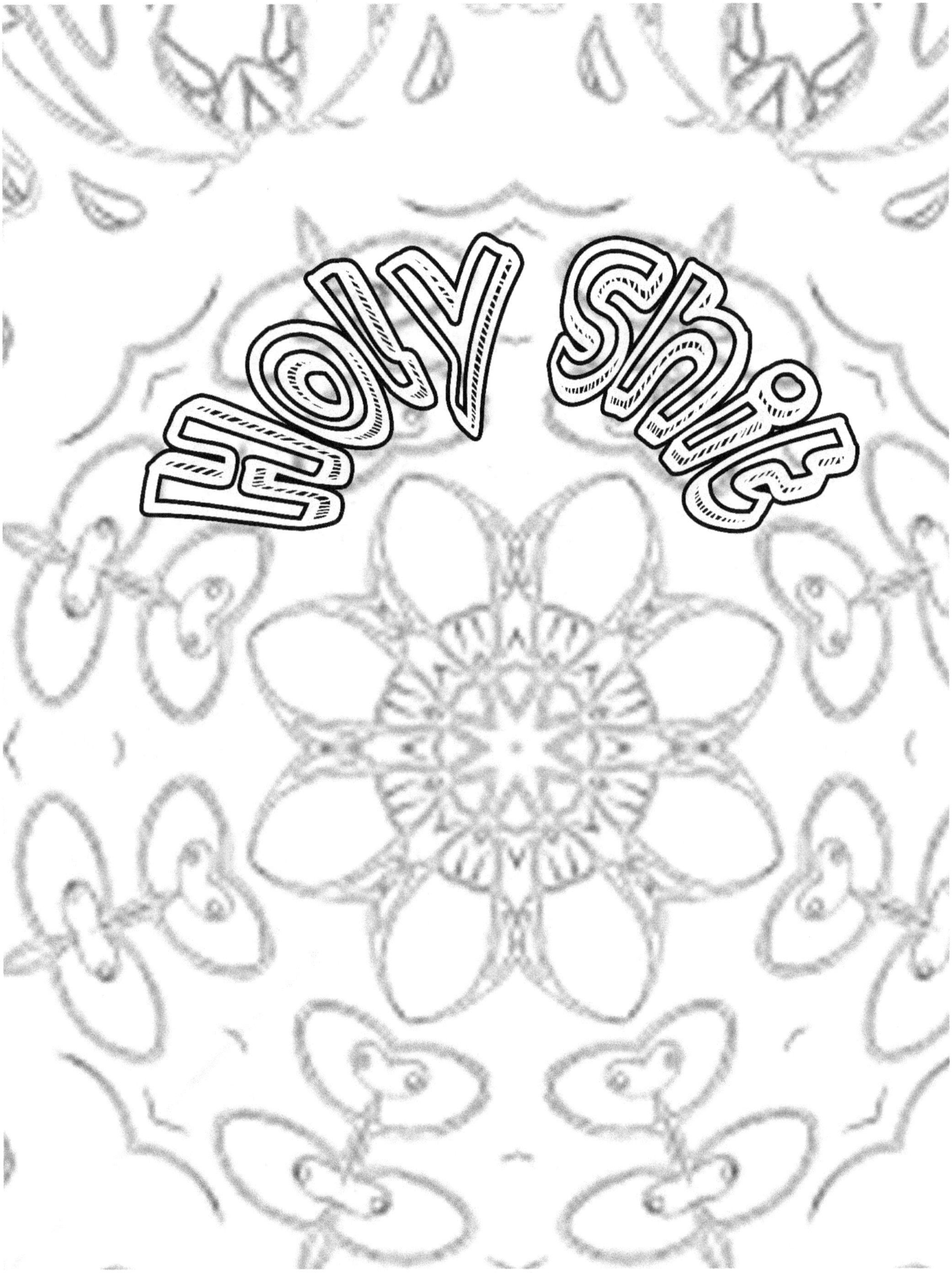
Holy Shit

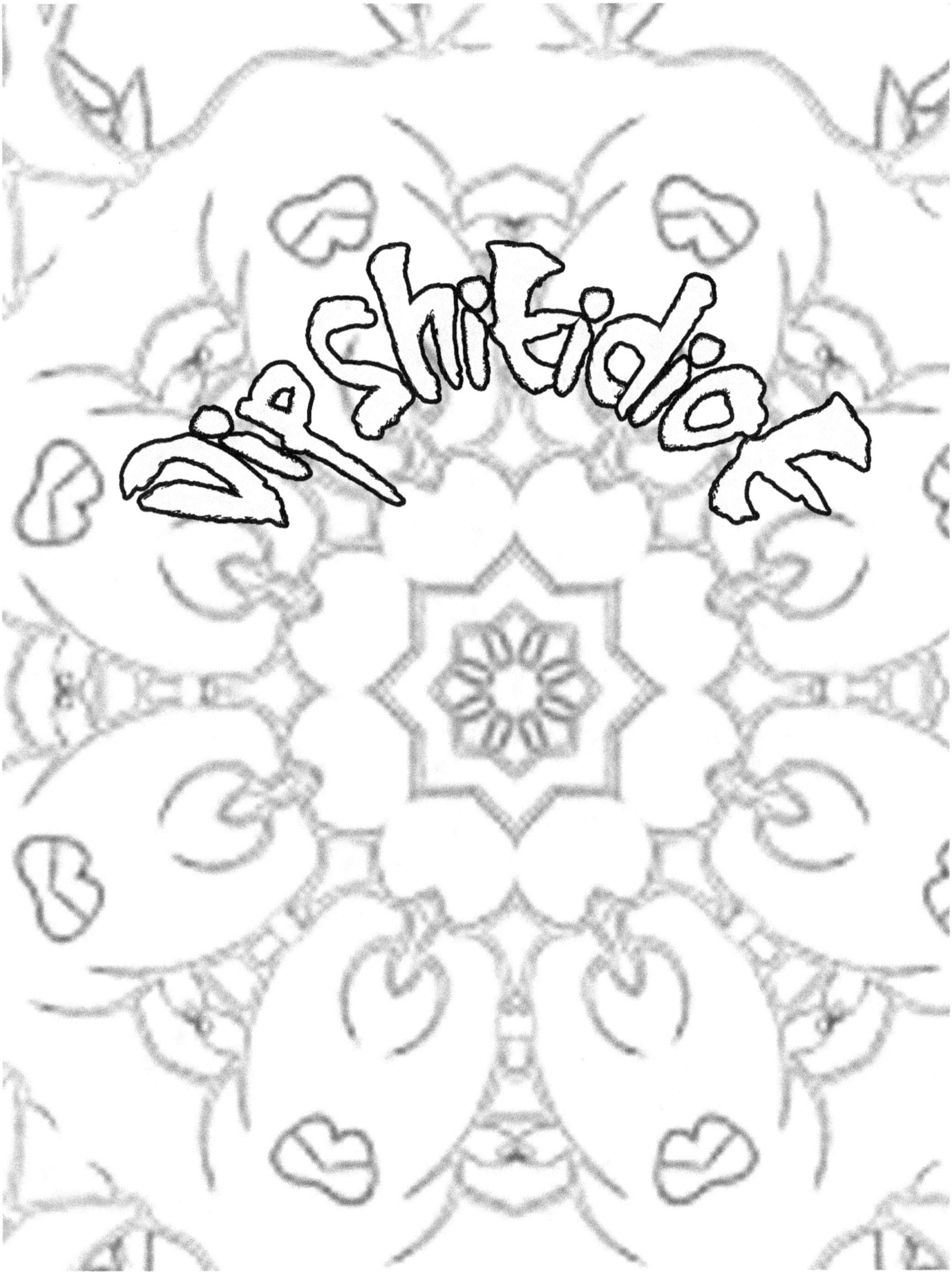
Dipshitidiot

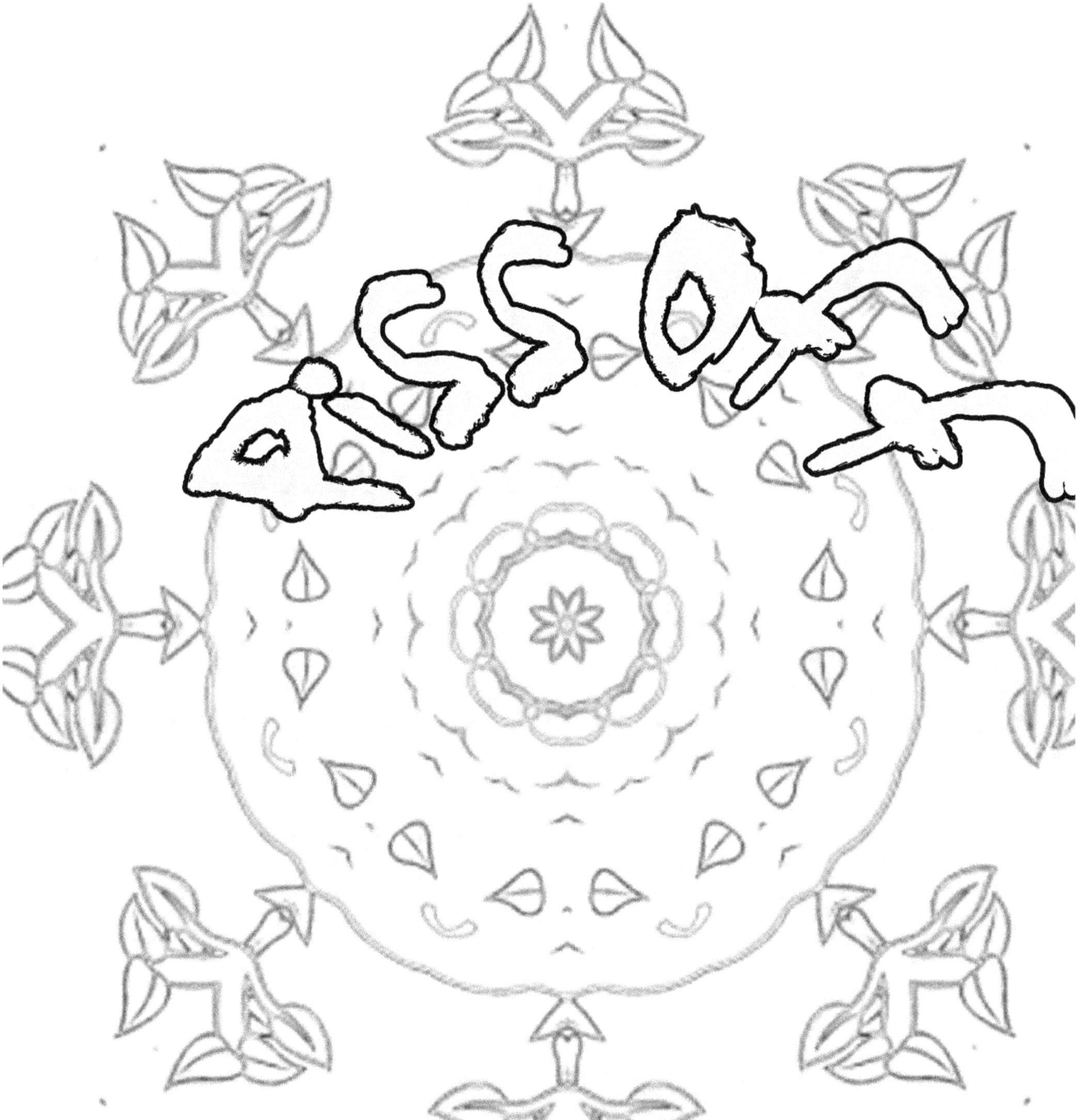
piss off

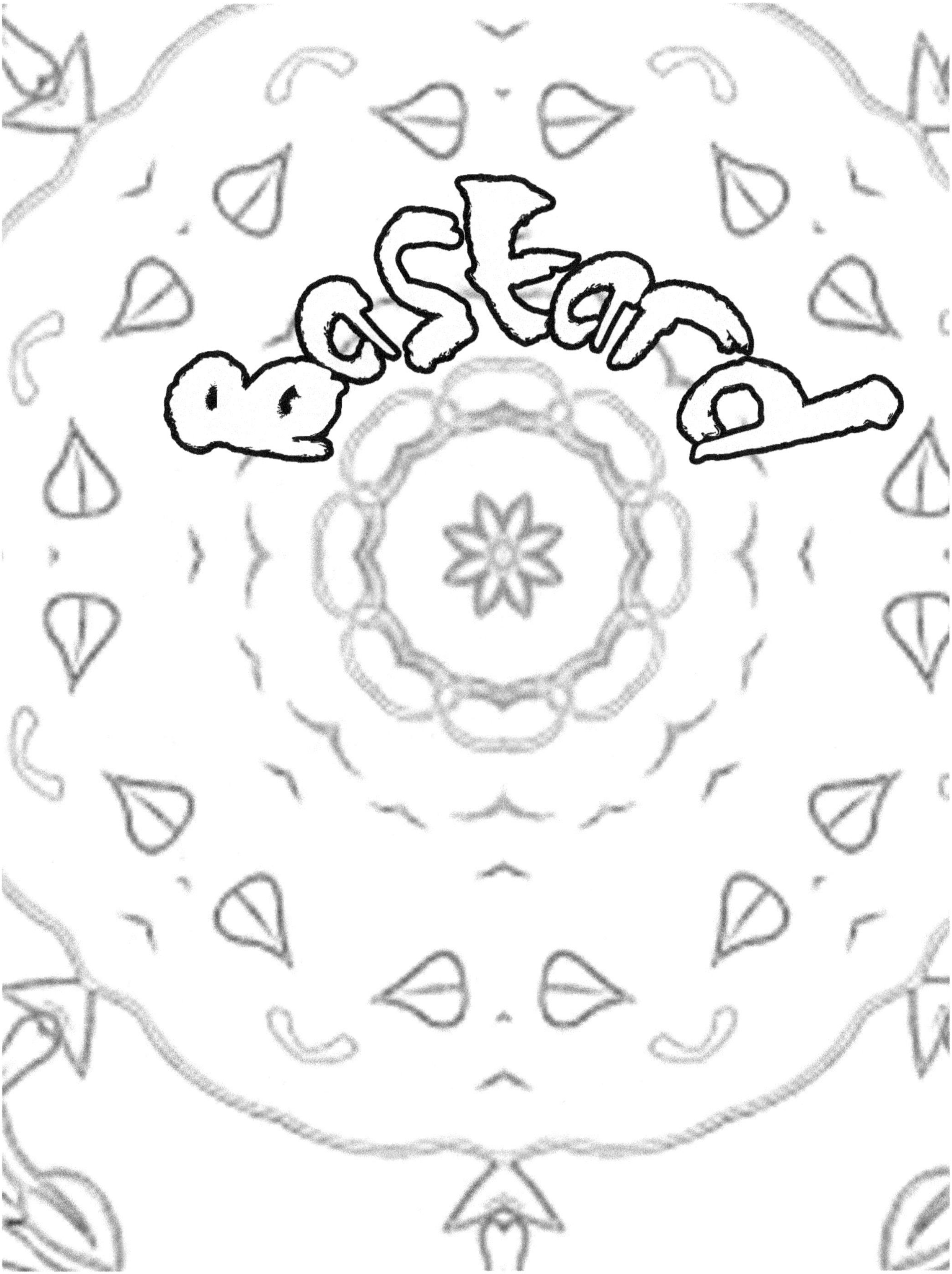
Bastard

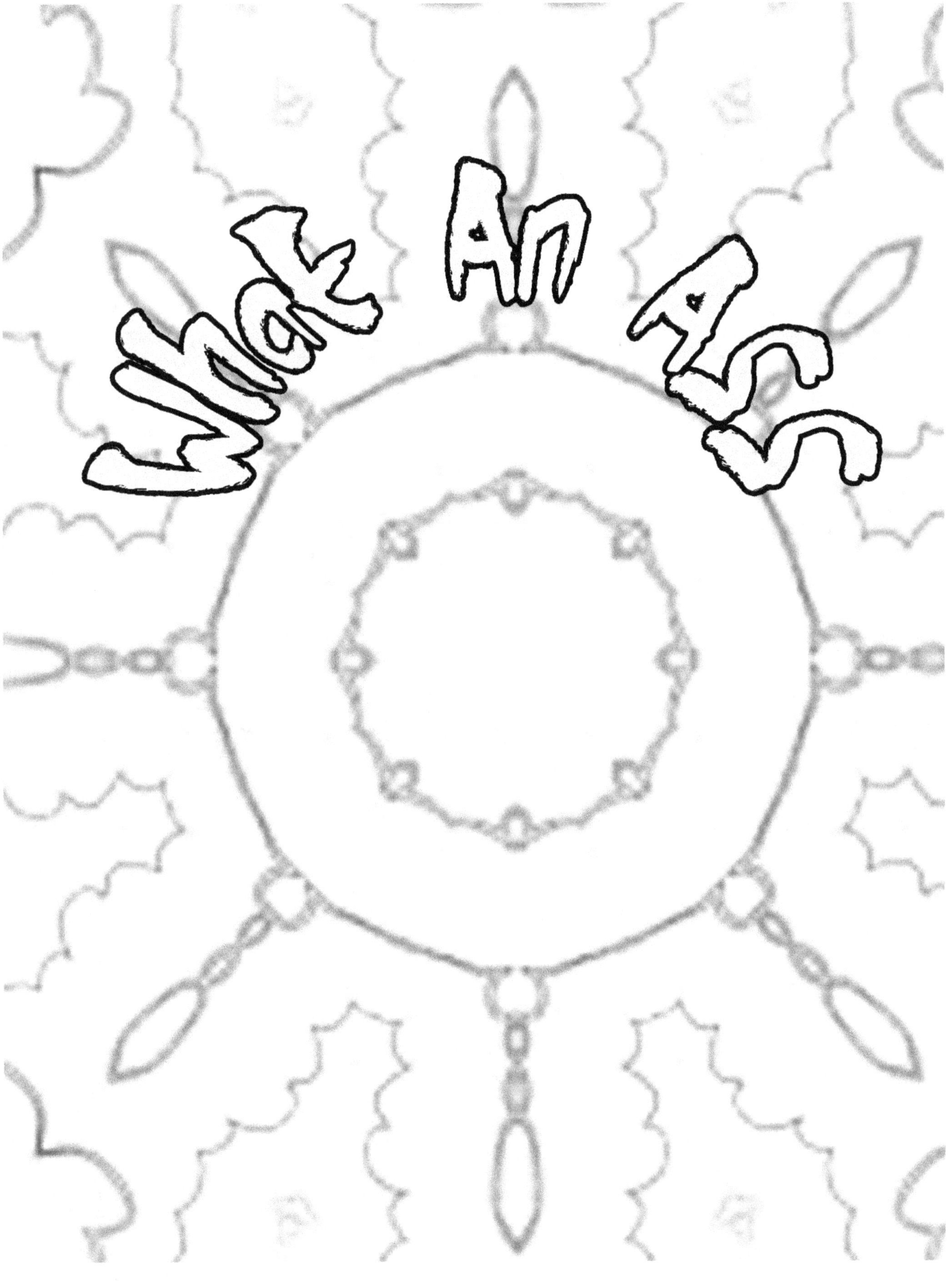
What An Ass

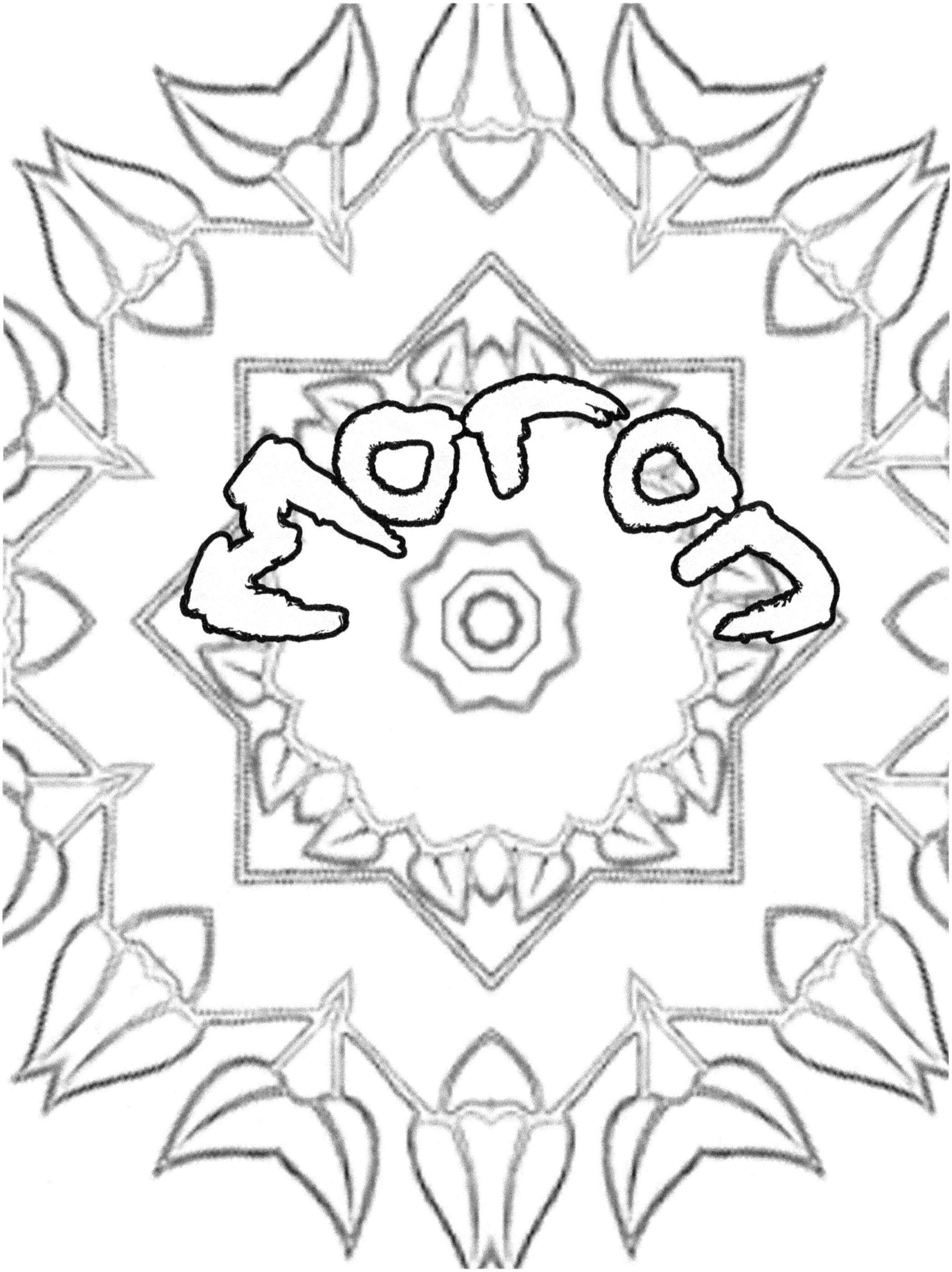

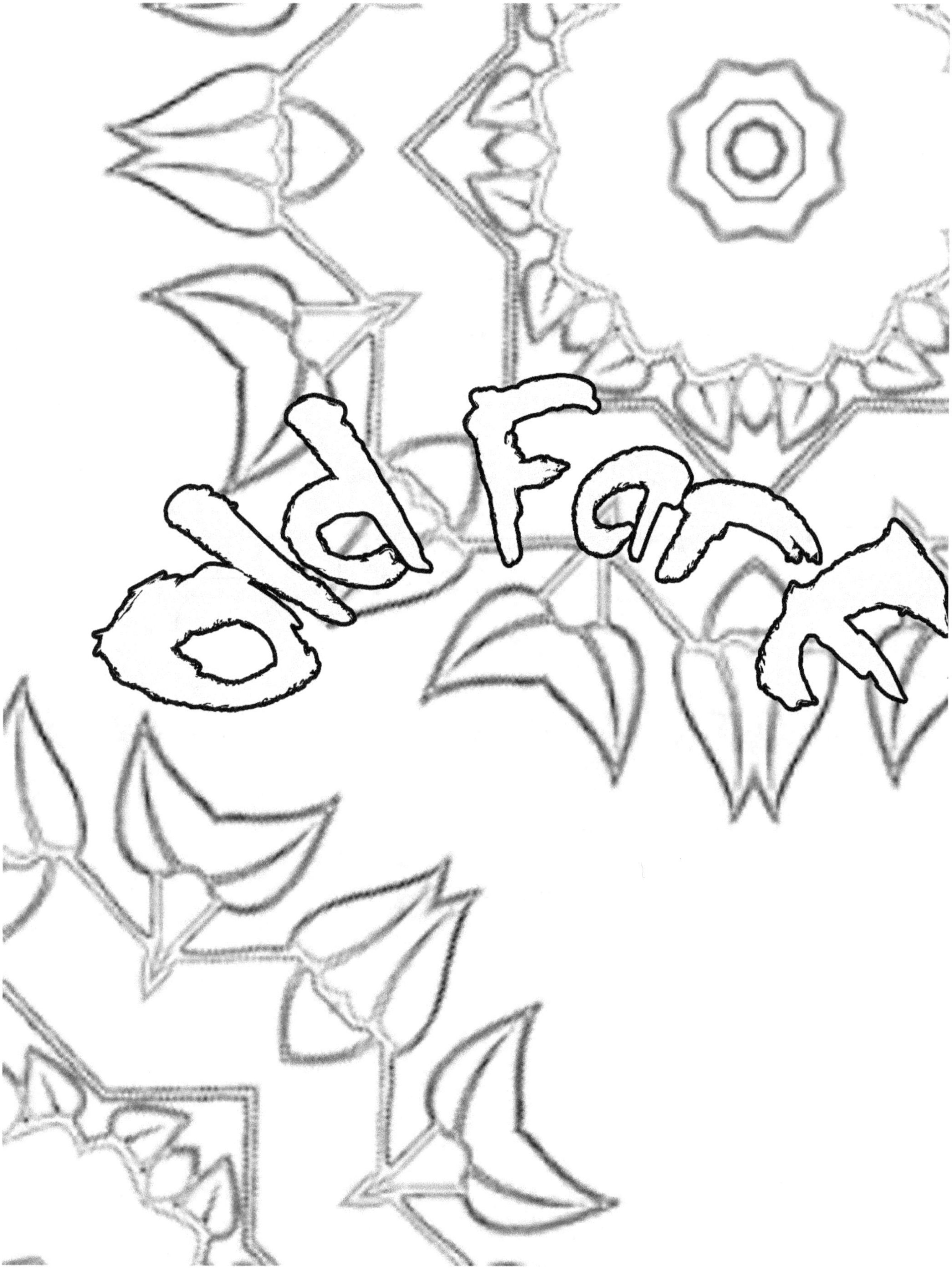
old Far

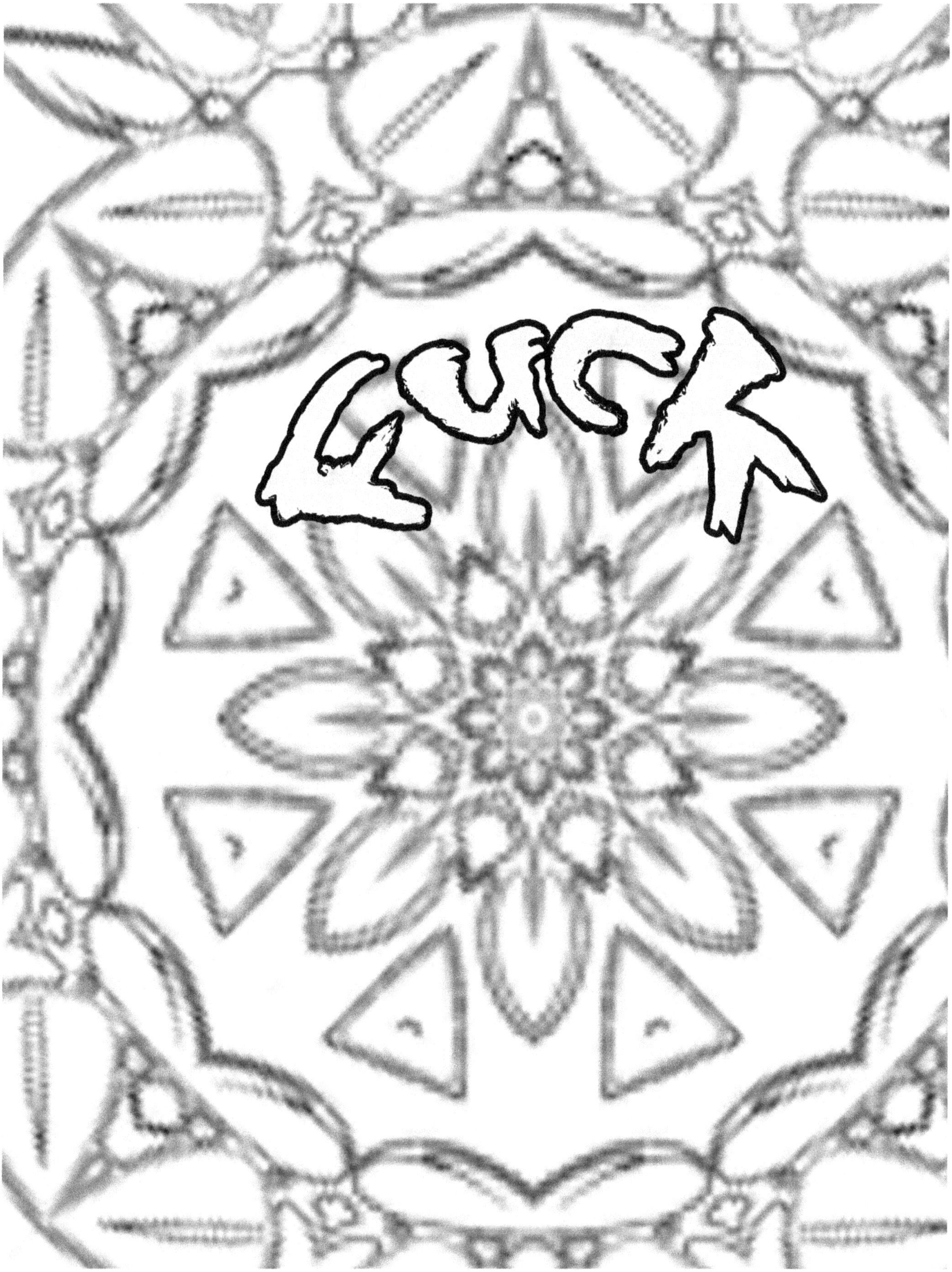
Fuck

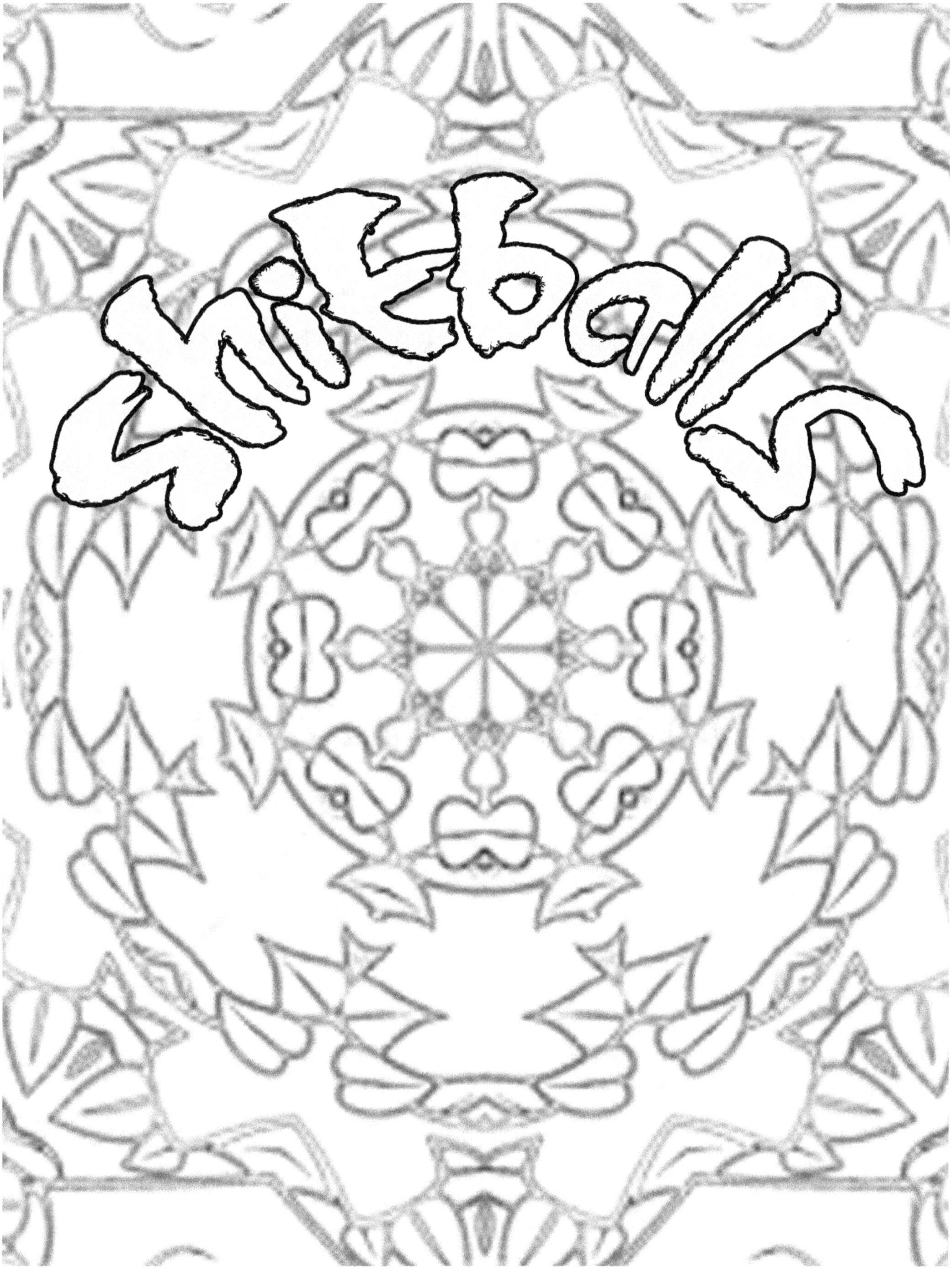
shitballs

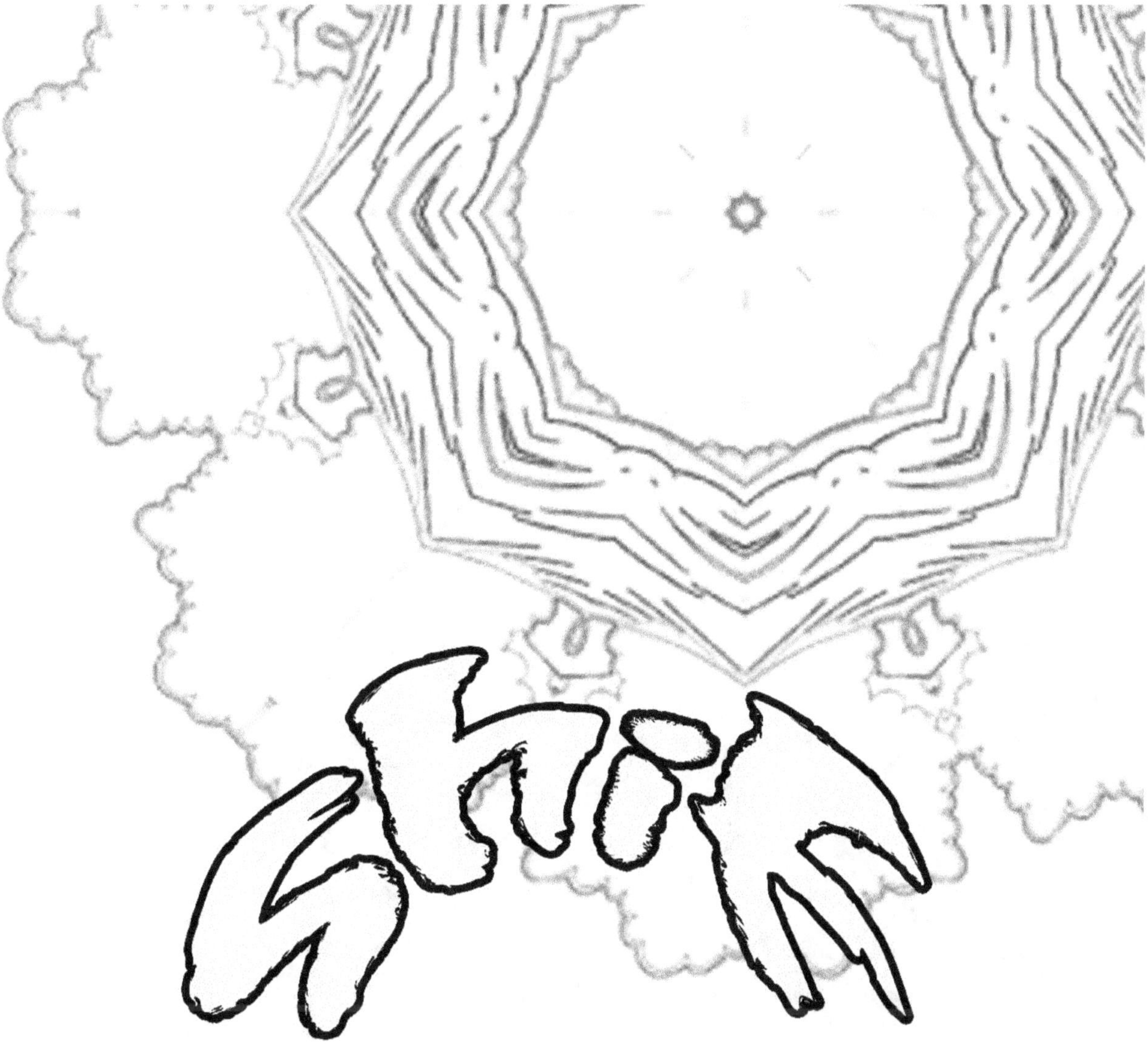
shim

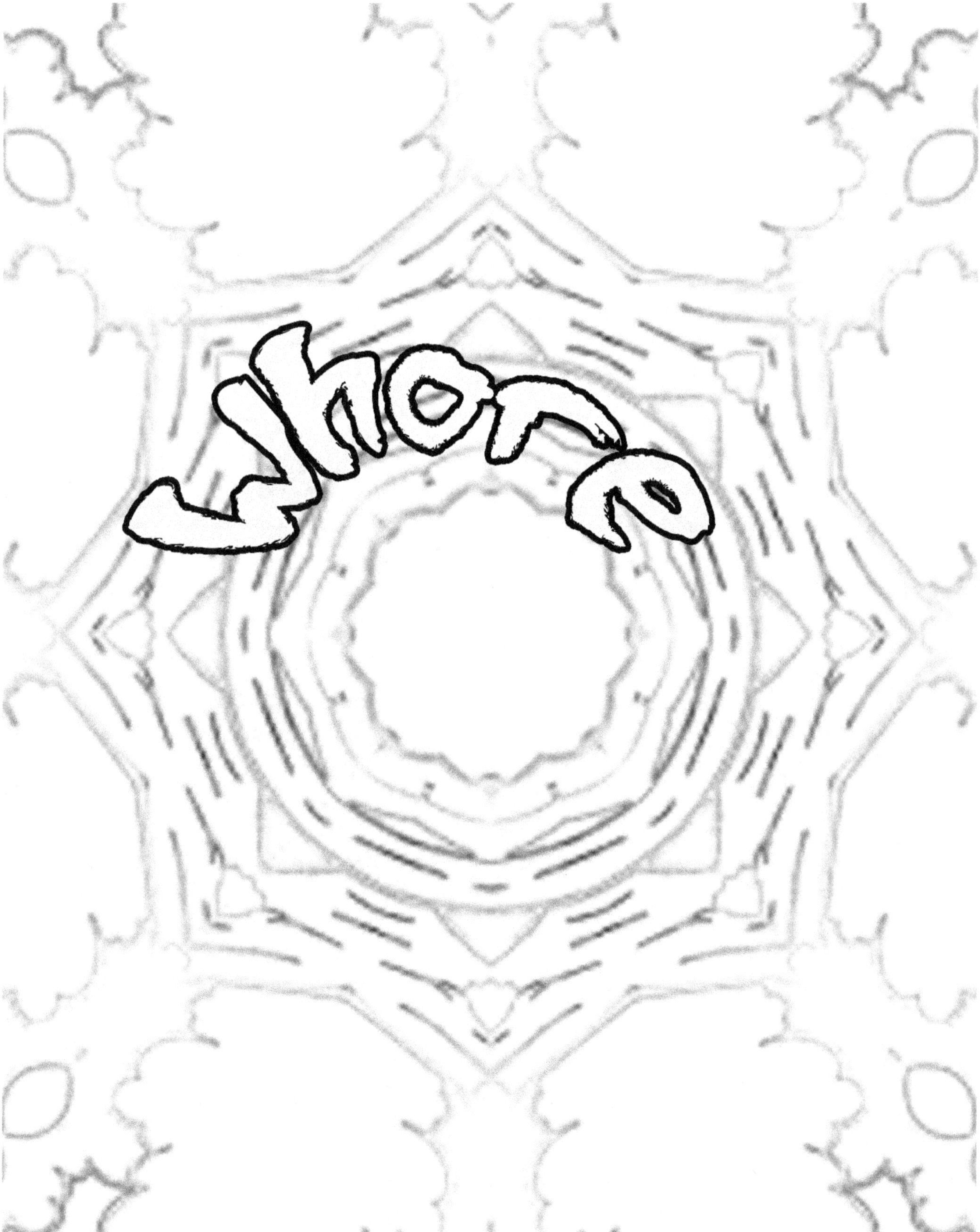
whore

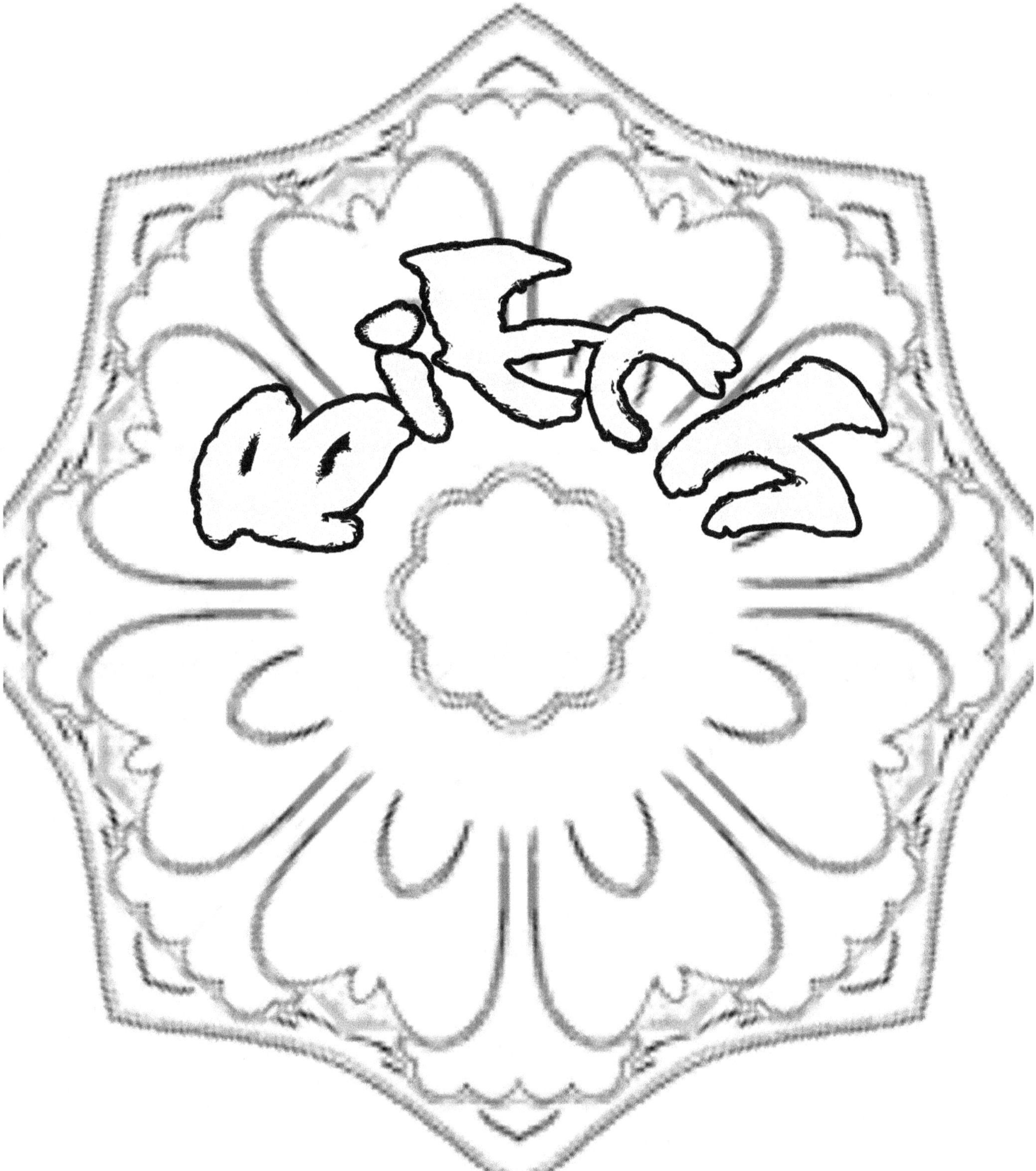
Bitch

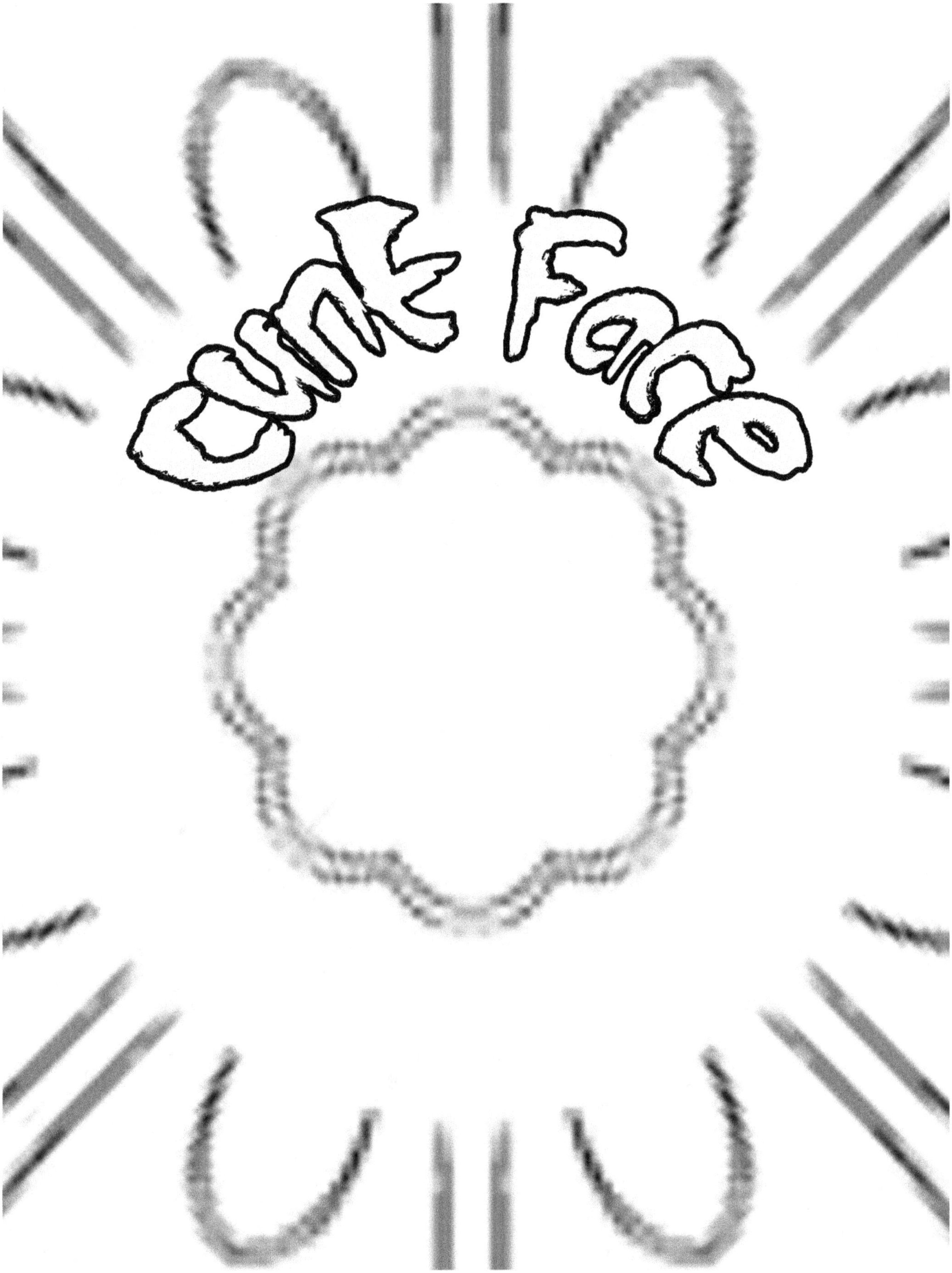
Cunt Face

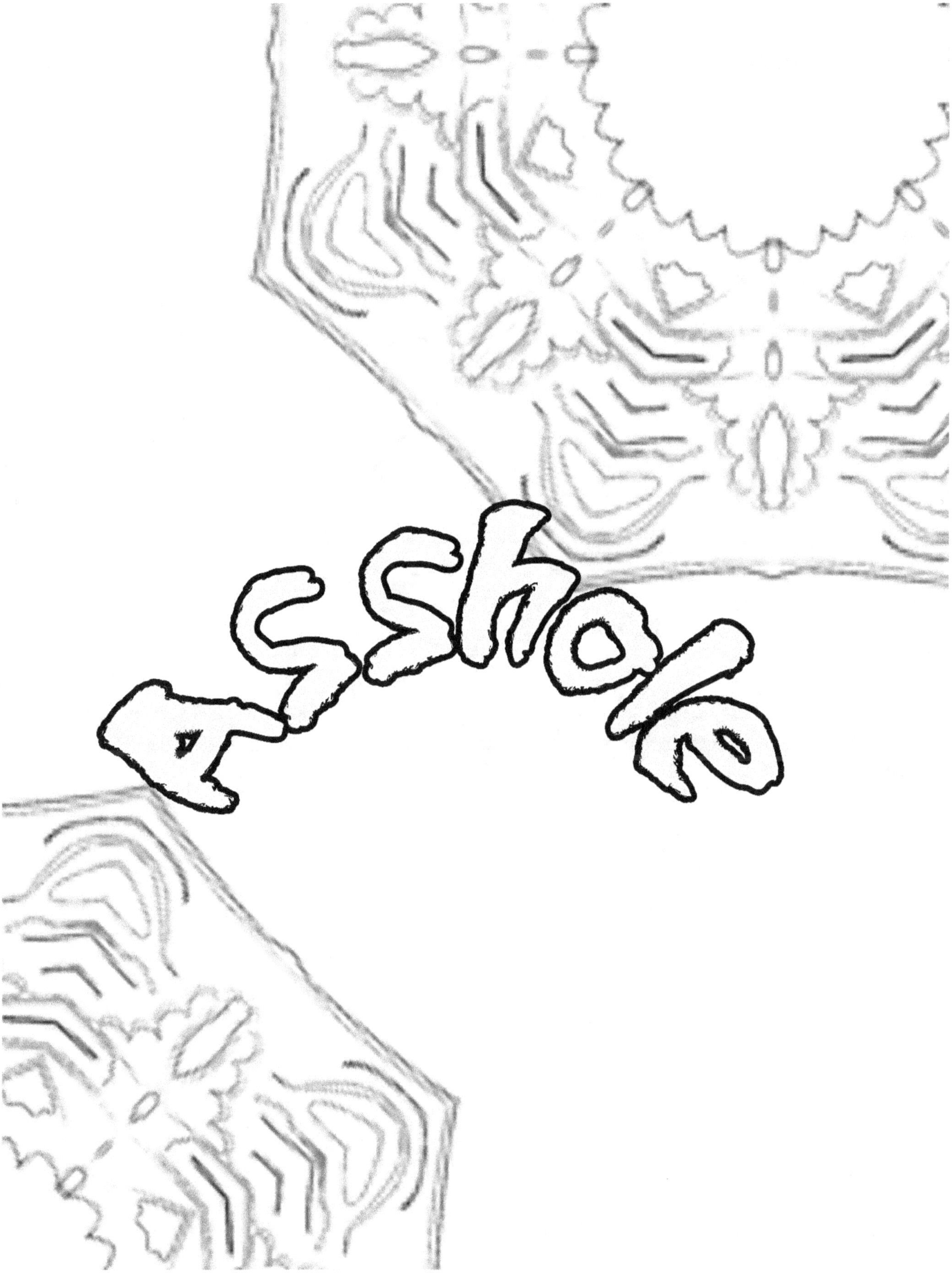
Asshole

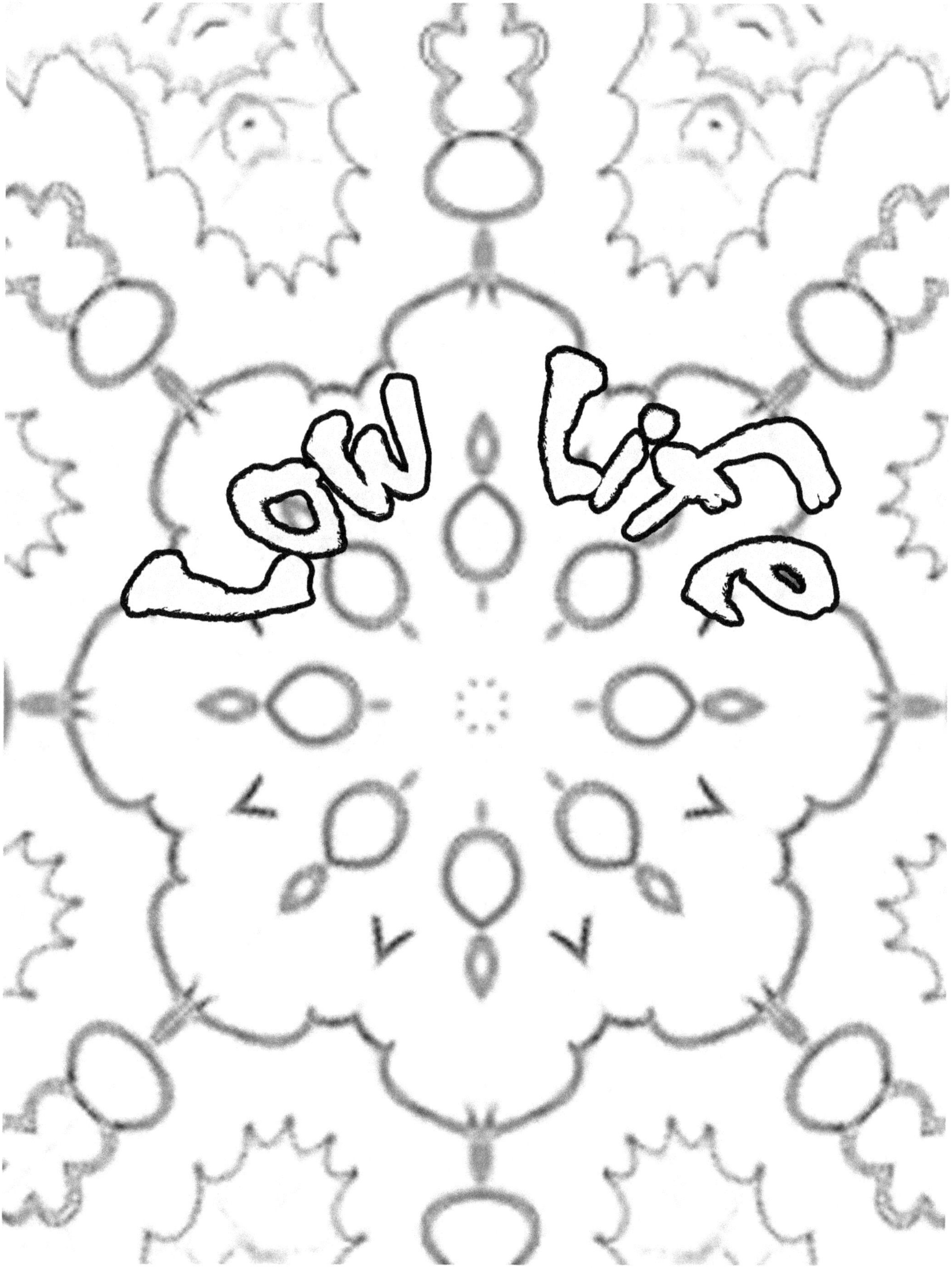
Low Life

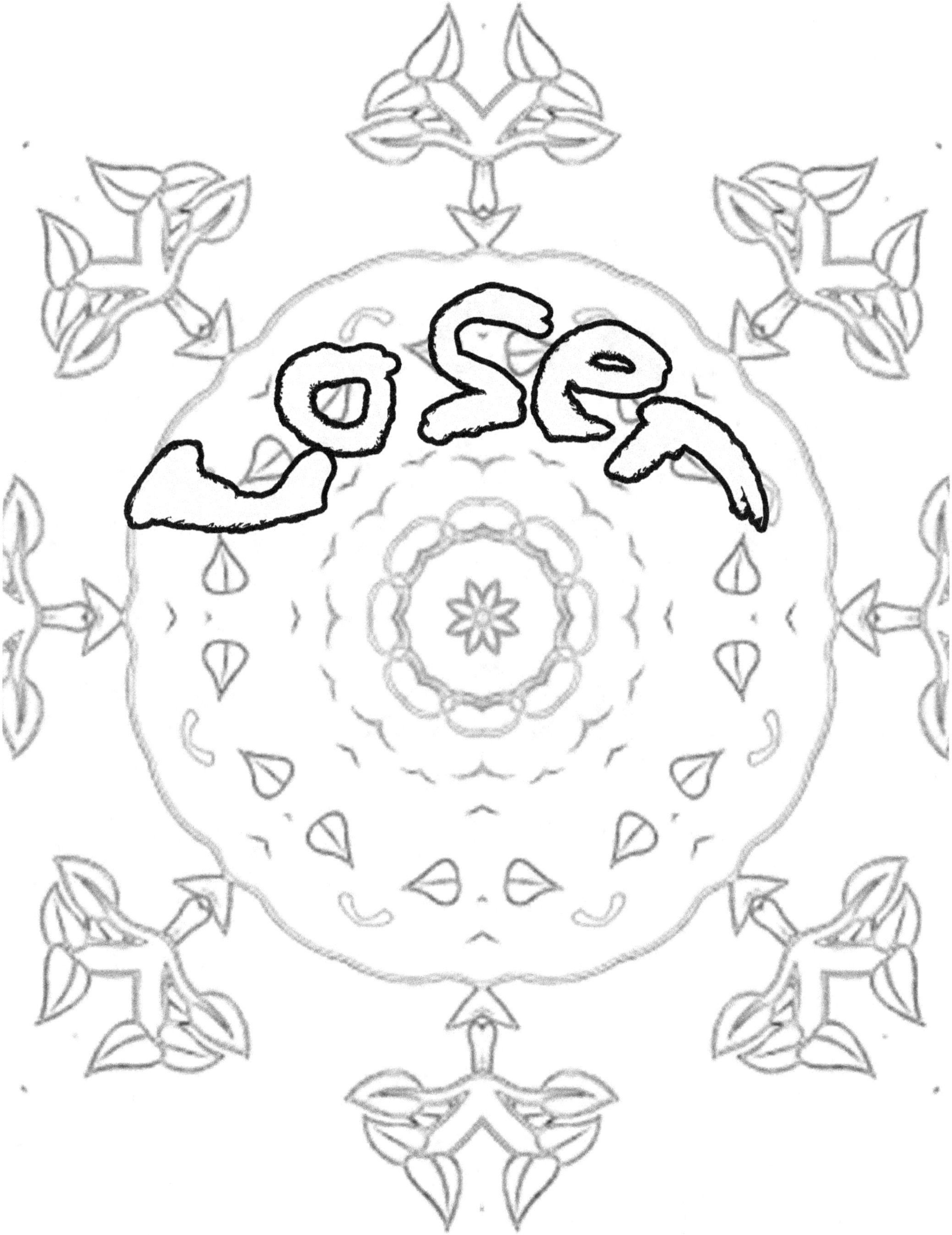
Loser

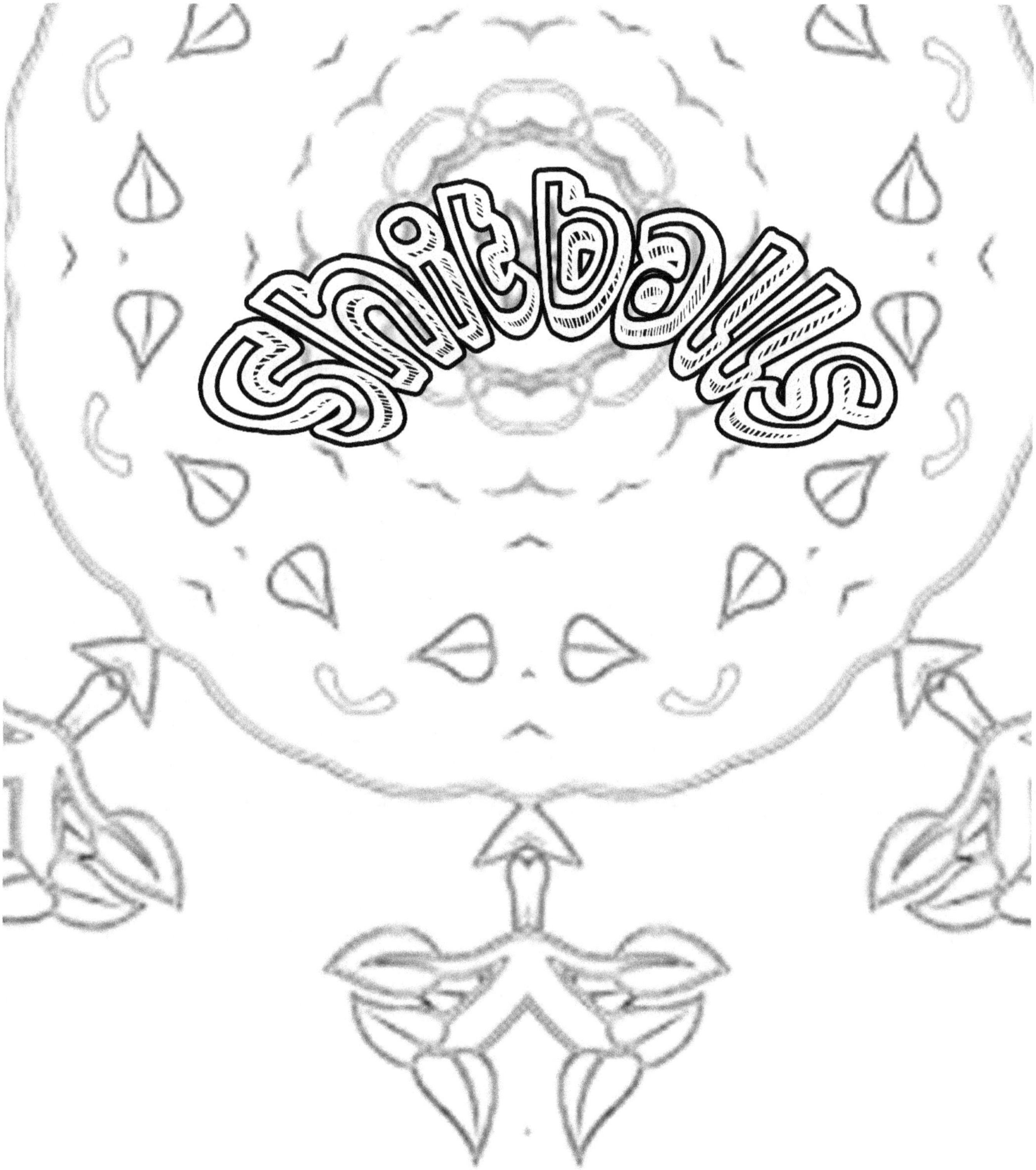
chitballs

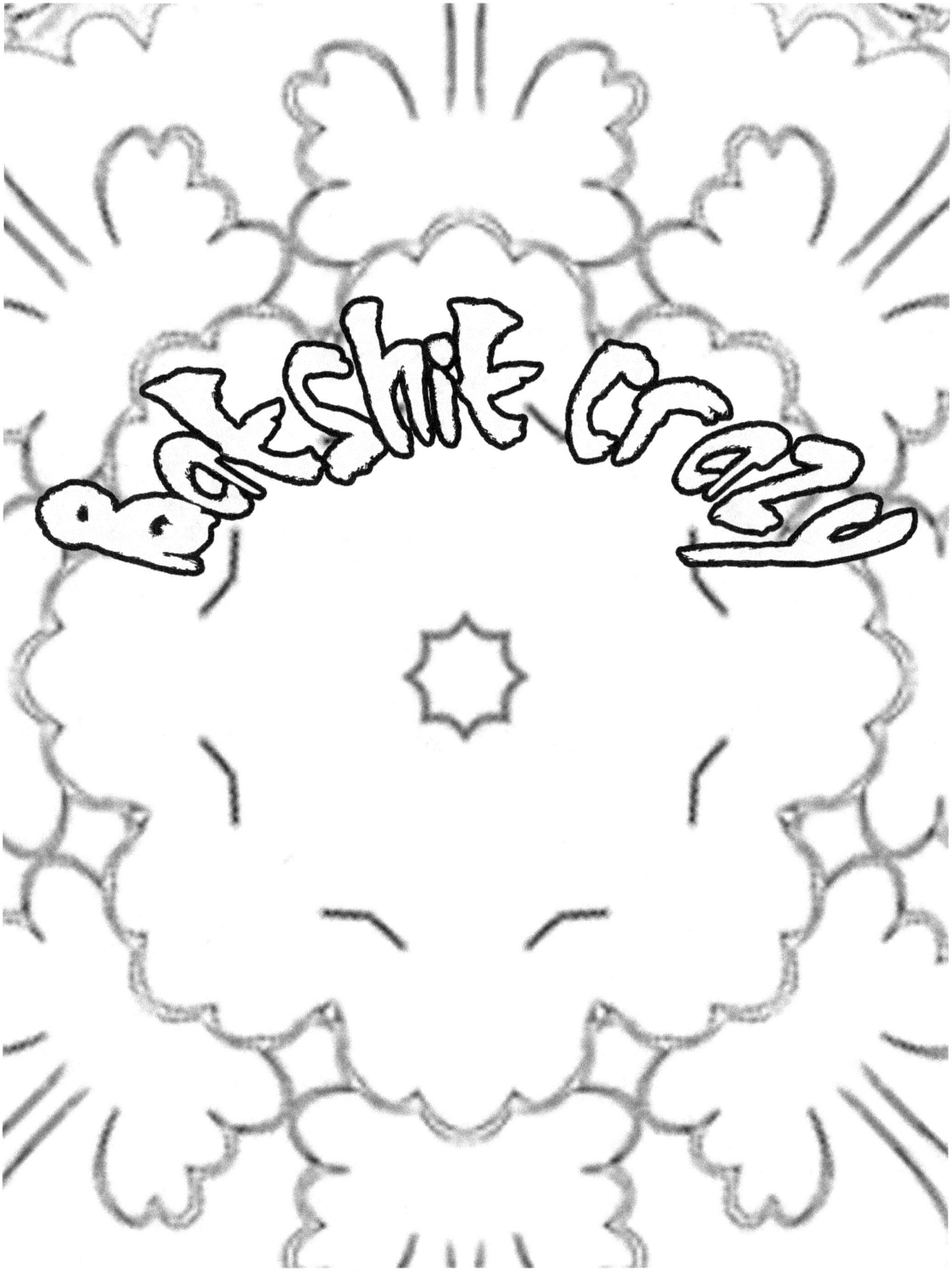
batshit crazy

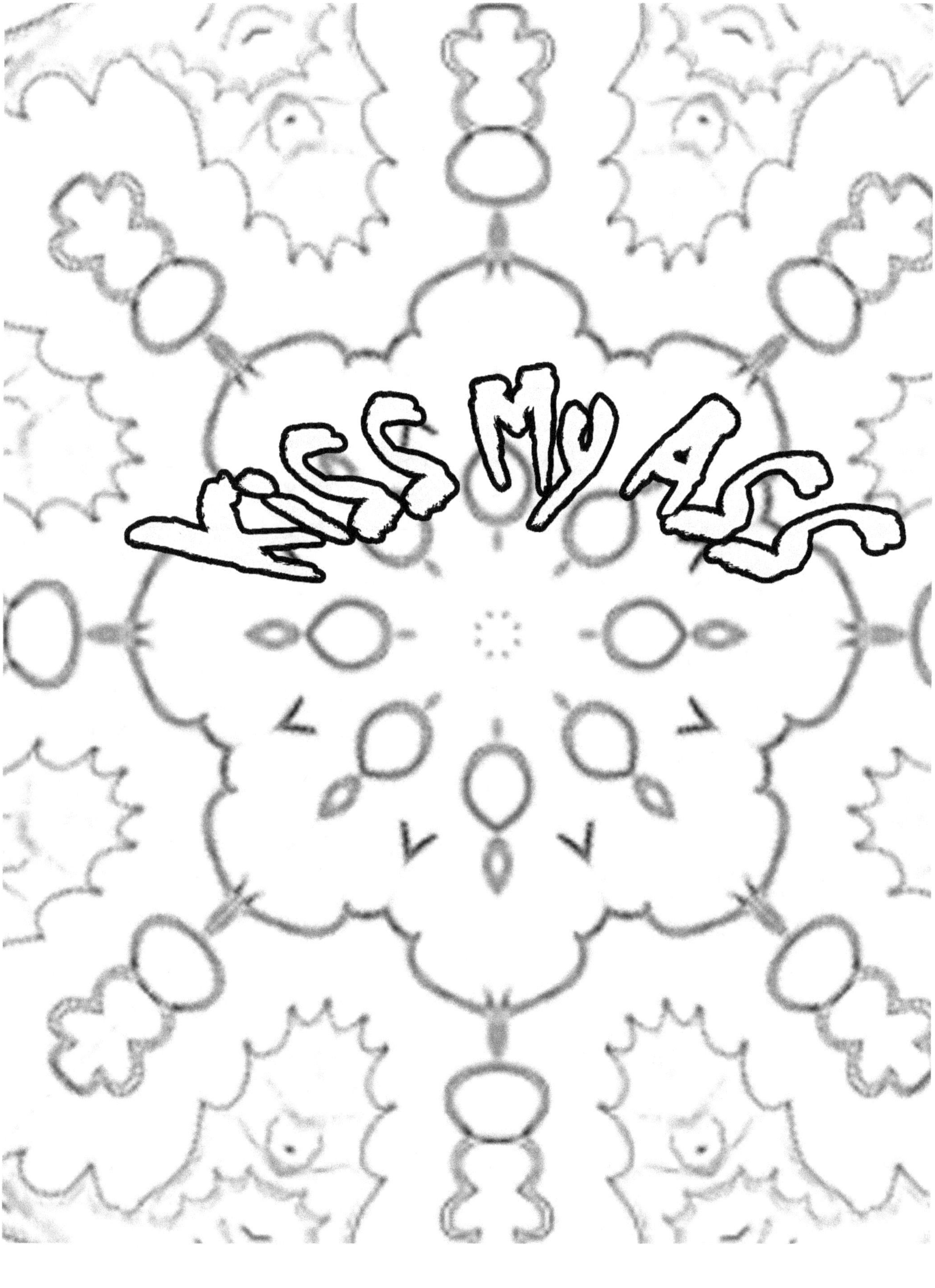
KISS MY ASS

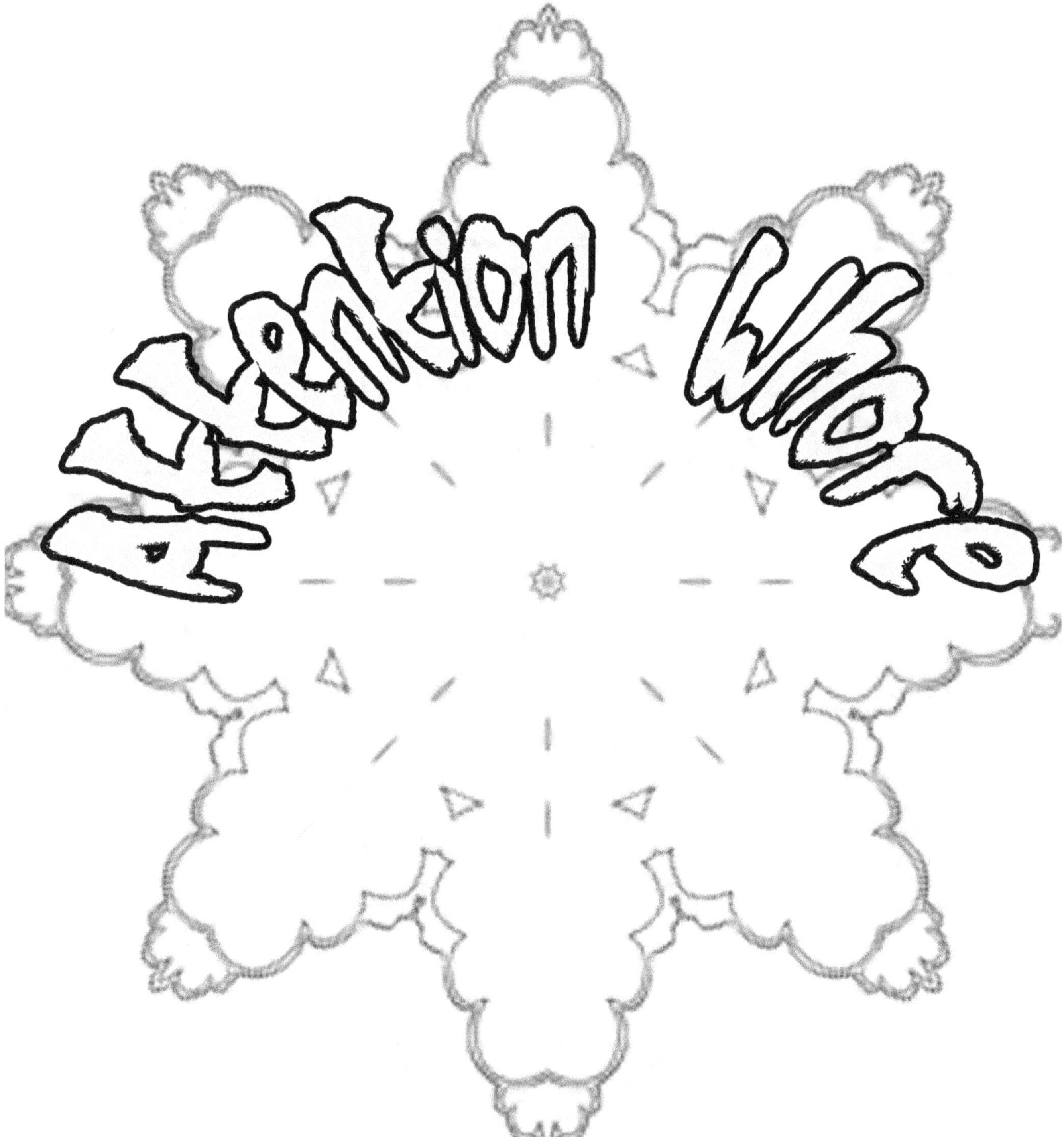
Attention Whore

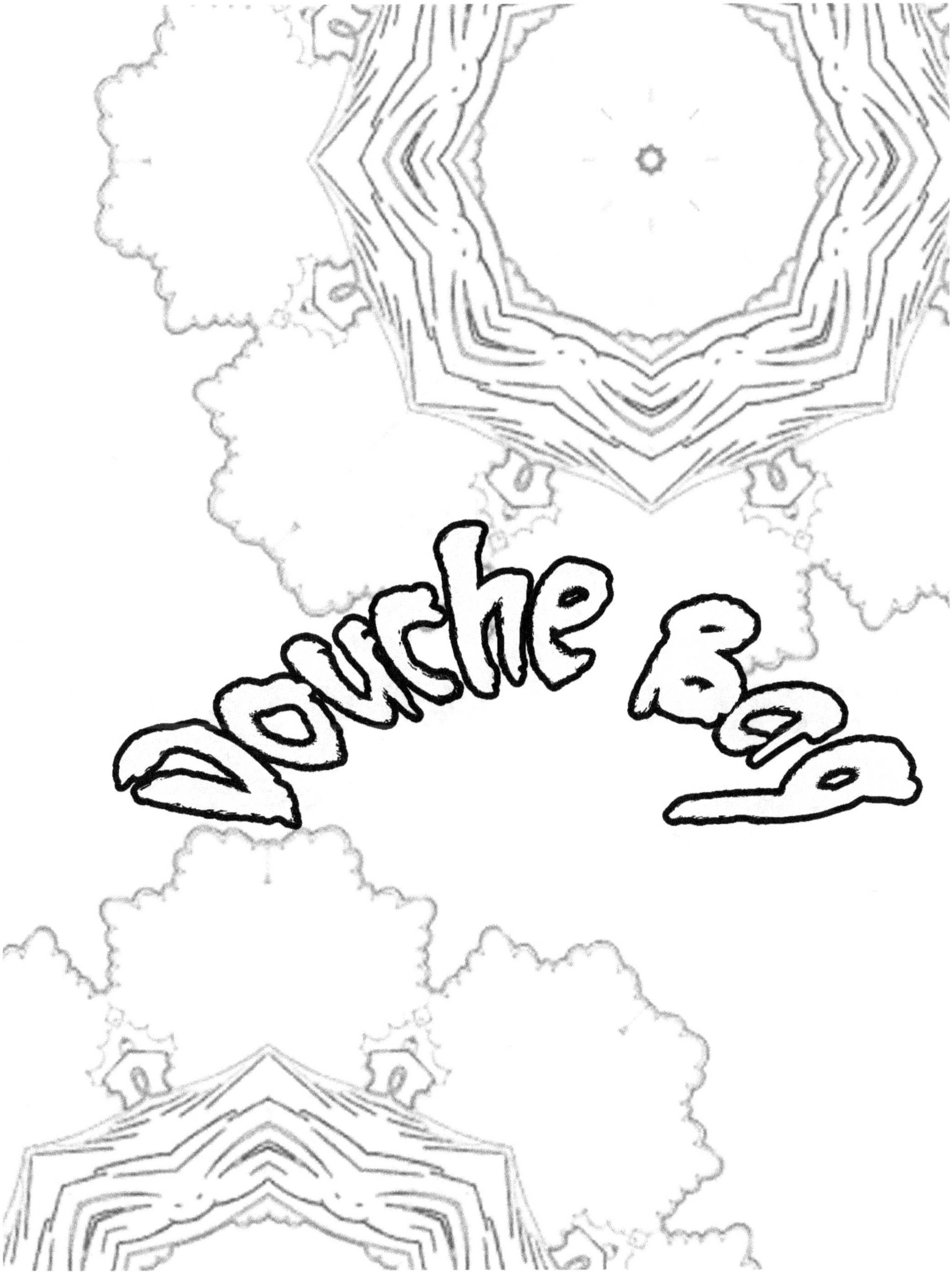
Douche Bag

www.ingramcontent.com/pod-product-compliance
Lightning Source LLC
Chambersburg PA
CBHW081747170526
45167CB00009B/3956
9781544087207